Creating Joy

A journal designed by Karina Duffy

All glory goes to my Lord

The Why

I was sitting in class, snacking on some dry cereal, when I listened to the conversations around me. My peers were ranting about how they are perpetually Stressed, Tired, and Depressed. (It's high school's very own STD.) I thought to myself how sad it is that so many are just going through the motions every day, living without zeal.

I have always been a stress-case, junior year especially bad. I felt like I had no control over my time, my friendships, and my schoolwork. I sustained the ability to find joy every day, but it was like pulling teeth.

I titled the journal *Creating Joy* instead of *Creating Happiness* because there is a significant difference between joy and happiness. Happiness comes from happenstance. It is a feeling; one you get when you experience something positive. Yet, joy is maintained when the negatives and struggles come. Joy is created. We can construct the days to be our own and take possession of the stresses and anxieties that haunt us.

This journal is my daily routine. I realized the worries that pulsed repeatedly in my mind were minuscule when I addressed them. My days are more fulfilling, and I go to bed joyful, rather than anxious about if I spent my time wisely.

Reasoning behind each section:

I start the log off with a quote from some of the world's greatest. It is there for you to contemplate and ponder.

When we start our mornings and end our night by identifying the blessings in our lives, we will have more peace and contentment versus jealousy of others. It is scientifically proven that just listing three good things about your day will increase life satisfaction.

While studying for the SAT, I watched videos, read books, and listened to podcasts to train my mind for the test day. It is a large mental game; if I could tone down my anxieties, I would be able to master the test. What I found was interesting - I must identify what was stressing me out and then come up with a solution. This gave me control over how to approach the hard problems and the so-called "test anxiety" I was having. I applied this concept to my daily life. When I imagine what I will be worried about and come up with a solution, I have more control over my day.

If we center our day focused on three things instead of a million, our days will be more fruitful. So instead of trying to change the world or yourself in one day, try to change a few things. For example, smile at someone new or say "I'm strong" every time you go to a mirror to empower yourself.

At night, the open space is there for you to reflect. Talk about your daily struggles, your triumphs, how you stuck or didn't stick to your goals.

I hope that this may make a change in your life just as it has in mine. I hope you will create joy in moments filled with both love and hardship. God bless☺

DATE: 01/07/19

IT'S NEVER TOO LATE TO BE WHAT YOU MIGHT HAVE BEEN — GEORGE ELIOT

Morning:

Three Moments of Gratitude:

1. Woke up without a headache

2. I am laying in a warm bed with fluffy sheets

3. Having best friends to laugh with at the game last night

Three Worries / Improvements:

1. Going to do poorly on my physics quiz - think about it as a way to check your process and do a few problems before to prep your brain

2. I will get in a bad mood for no apparent reason and take it out on others - take a deep breath and tell yourself that you are in control of your feelings

3. I will get a headache - drink lots of water, take pills if needed, and smile more

Three Things to Accomplish (Mentally or Physically):

1. Buy the person behind you a drink at Starbucks

2. When you feel self-conscious tell yourself that you are incomparable

3. Find beauty in three things today (If one is a person, compliment them!)

Night:

Open Space: (I'm not going to model it because it is an infinite space to write about whatever your heart desires to write about)

_____

_____

_____

_____

_____

_____

_____

_____

_____

_____

_____

_____

_____

_____

_____

_____

_____

_____

_____

Three Moments of Gratitude:

1. I completed a new and difficult workout

2. Got to eat dinner with my family

3. I have a shower that I can use whenever I want

DATE:

YOU GET IN LIFE WHAT YOU HAVE THE COURAGE TO ASK FOR — NANCY D. SOLOMON

Morning:

Three Moments of Gratitude:

1._____

2._____

3._____

Three Worries / Improvements:

1._____

_____

2._____

_____

3._____

_____

Three Things to Accomplish (Mentally or Physically):

1._____

2._____

3._____

Night:

Open Space:

_____

_____

_____

_____

_____

_____

_____

_____

_____

_____

_____

_____

_____

_____

_____

_____

_____

_____

Three Moments of Gratitude:

1._____

2._____

3._____

DATE:

SUCCESS CONSISTS OF GOING FROM FAILURE TO FAILURE WITHOUT LOSS OF ENTHUSIASM – WINSTON CHIURCHILL

Morning:

Three Moments of Gratitude:

1._____

2._____

3._____

Three Worries / Improvements:

1._____

_____

2._____

_____

3._____

_____

Three Things to Accomplish (Mentally or Physically):

1._____

2._____

3._____

Night:

Open Space:

_____

_____

_____

_____

_____

_____

_____

_____

_____

_____

_____

_____

_____

_____

_____

_____

_____

_____

_____

Three Moments of Gratitude:

1._____

2._____

3._____

DATE:

ALL YOU NEED IN THIS LIFE IGNORANCE AND CONFIDENCE, AND THEN SUCCESS IS SURE — MARK TWAIN

Morning:

Three Moments of Gratitude:

1._____

2._____

3._____

Three Worries / Improvements:

1._____

_____

2._____

_____

3._____

_____

Three Things to Accomplish (Mentally or Physically):

1._____

2._____

3._____

Night:

Open Space:

_____

_____

_____

_____

_____

_____

_____

_____

_____

_____

_____

_____

_____

_____

_____

_____

_____

_____

_____

Three Moments of Gratitude:

1._____

2._____

3._____

DATE:

EVER TRIED. EVER FAILED. NO MATTER. TRY AGAIN. FAIL AGAIN. FAIL BETTER. — SAMUEL BECKETT

Morning:

Three Moments of Gratitude:

1._____

2._____

3._____

Three Worries / Improvements:

1._____

_____

2._____

_____

3._____

_____

Three Things to Accomplish (Mentally or Physically):

1._____

2._____

3._____

Night:

Open Space:

_____

_____

_____

_____

_____

_____

_____

_____

_____

_____

_____

_____

_____

_____

_____

_____

_____

Three Moments of Gratitude:

1._____

2._____

3._____

DATE:

IF YOU'RE GOING THROUGH HELL, KEEP GOING. — WINSTON CHURCHILL

Morning:

Three Moments of Gratitude:

1._____

2._____

3._____

Three Worries / Improvements:

1._____

_____

2._____

_____

3._____

_____

Three Things to Accomplish (Mentally or Physically):

1._____

2._____

3._____

Night:

Open Space:

_____

_____

_____

_____

_____

_____

_____

_____

_____

_____

_____

_____

_____

_____

_____

_____

_____

_____

_____

Three Moments of Gratitude:

1._____

2._____

3._____

DATE:

WE AREN'T GOOD OR BAD AT ANYTHING WE HAVEN'T TRIED — MELISSA ARNOT

Morning:

Three Moments of Gratitude:

1._____

2._____

3._____

Three Worries / Improvements:

1._____

_____

2._____

_____

3._____

_____

Three Things to Accomplish (Mentally or Physically):

1._____

2._____

3._____

Night:

Open Space:

_____

_____

_____

_____

_____

_____

_____

_____

_____

_____

_____

_____

_____

_____

_____

_____

_____

_____

Three Moments of Gratitude:

1._____

2._____

3._____

DATE:

IT'S A SAD DAY WHEN YOU FIND OUT THAT IT'S NOT ACCIDENT OR FORTUNE BUT JUST YOURSELF THAT KEPT THINGS FROM YOU — LILLIAN HELLMAN

Morning:

Three Moments of Gratitude:

1._____

2._____

3._____

Three Worries / Improvements:

1._____

_____

2._____

_____

3._____

_____

Three Things to Accomplish (Mentally or Physically):

1._____

2._____

3._____

Night:

Open Space:

_____

_____

_____

_____

_____

_____

_____

_____

_____

_____

_____

_____

_____

_____

_____

_____

_____

_____

Three Moments of Gratitude:

1._____

2._____

3._____

DATE:

YOUR ASSUMPTIONS ARE YOUR WINDOWS ON THE WORLD. SCRUB THEM OFF EVERY ONCE IN A WHILE, OR THE LIGHT WON'T COME IN — ALAN ALDA

Morning:

Three Moments of Gratitude:

1._____

2._____

3._____

Three Worries / Improvements:

1._____

_____

2._____

_____

3._____

_____

Three Things to Accomplish (Mentally or Physically):

1._____

2._____

3._____

Night:

Open Space:

_____

_____

_____

_____

_____

_____

_____

_____

_____

_____

_____

_____

_____

_____

_____

_____

_____

_____

Three Moments of Gratitude:

1._____

2._____

3._____

DATE:

ALWAYS GO WITH THE CHOICE THAT SCARES YOU THE MOST, BECAUSE THAT'S THE ONE THAT IS GOING TO REQUIRE THE MOST FROM YOU — CAROLINE MYSS

Morning:

Three Moments of Gratitude:

1._____

2._____

3._____

Three Worries / Improvements:

1._____

_____

2._____

_____

3._____

_____

Three Things to Accomplish (Mentally or Physically):

1._____

2._____

3._____

Night:

Open Space:

_____

_____

_____

_____

_____

_____

_____

_____

_____

_____

_____

_____

_____

_____

_____

_____

_____

_____

Three Moments of Gratitude:

1._____

2._____

3._____

DATE:

DO NOT MIND ANYTHING THAT ANYONE TELLS YOU ABOUT ANYONE ELSE. JUDGE EVERYONE AND EVERYTHING FOR YOURSELF – HENRY JAMES

Morning:

Three Moments of Gratitude:

1._____

2._____

3._____

Three Worries / Improvements:

1._____

_____

2._____

_____

3._____

_____

Three Things to Accomplish (Mentally or Physically):

1._____

2._____

3._____

Night:

Open Space:

_____

_____

_____

_____

_____

_____

_____

_____

_____

_____

_____

_____

_____

_____

_____

_____

_____

Three Moments of Gratitude:

1._____

2._____

3._____

DATE:

**I KNOW FOR SURE THAT WHAT WE DWELL ON IS WHO WE BECOME —
OPRAH WINFREY**

Morning:

Three Moments of Gratitude:

1._____

2._____

3._____

Three Worries / Improvements:

1._____

_____

2._____

_____

3._____

_____

Three Things to Accomplish (Mentally or Physically):

1._____

2._____

3._____

Night:

Open Space:

_____

_____

_____

_____

_____

_____

_____

_____

_____

_____

_____

_____

_____

_____

_____

_____

_____

_____

Three Moments of Gratitude:

1._____

2._____

3._____

DATE:

VERY OFTEN A CHANGE OF SELF IS NEEDED MORE THAN A CHANGE OF SCENE — ARTHUR CHRISTOPHER BENSON

Morning:

Three Moments of Gratitude:

1._____

2._____

3._____

Three Worries / Improvements:

1._____

_____

2._____

_____

3._____

_____

Three Things to Accomplish (Mentally or Physically):

1._____

2._____

3._____

Night:

Open Space:

_____

_____

_____

_____

_____

_____

_____

_____

_____

_____

_____

_____

_____

_____

_____

_____

_____

_____

_____

Three Moments of Gratitude:

1._____

2._____

3._____

DATE:

DO NOT DWELL IN THE PAST, DO NOT DREAM OF THE FUTURE, CONCENTRATE THE MIND ON THE PRESENT MOMENT - BUDDHA

Morning:

Three Moments of Gratitude:

1._____

2._____

3._____

Three Worries / Improvements:

1._____

_____

2._____

_____

3._____

_____

Three Things to Accomplish (Mentally or Physically):

1._____

2._____

3._____

Night:

Open Space:

_____

_____

_____

_____

_____

_____

_____

_____

_____

_____

_____

_____

_____

_____

_____

_____

_____

_____

Three Moments of Gratitude:

1._____

2._____

3._____

DATE:

THE MOST COMMON WAY PEOPLE GIVE UP THEIR POWER IS BY THINKING THEY DON'T HAVE ANY — ALICE WALKER

Morning:

Three Moments of Gratitude:

1._____

2._____

3._____

Three Worries / Improvements:

1._____

_____

2._____

_____

3._____

_____

Three Things to Accomplish (Mentally or Physically):

1._____

2._____

3._____

Night:

Open Space:

_____

_____

_____

_____

_____

_____

_____

_____

_____

_____

_____

_____

_____

_____

_____

_____

_____

_____

Three Moments of Gratitude:

1._____

2._____

3._____

DATE:

EXPECT THE UNEXPECTED, AND WHENEVER POSSIBLE, BE THE UNEXPECTED — LYNDA BERRY

Morning:

Three Moments of Gratitude:

1._____

2._____

3._____

Three Worries / Improvements:

1._____

_____

2._____

_____

3._____

_____

Three Things to Accomplish (Mentally or Physically):

1._____

2._____

3._____

Night:

Open Space:

_____

_____

_____

_____

_____

_____

_____

_____

_____

_____

_____

_____

_____

_____

_____

_____

_____

_____

Three Moments of Gratitude:

1._____

2._____

3._____

DATE:

LIFE IS 10% WHAT HAPPENS TO ME AND 90% OF HOW I REACT TO IT — CHARLES SWINDOLL

Morning:

Three Moments of Gratitude:

1._____

2._____

3._____

Three Worries / Improvements:

1._____

_____

2._____

_____

3._____

_____

Three Things to Accomplish (Mentally or Physically):

1._____

2._____

3._____

Night:

Open Space:

_____

_____

_____

_____

_____

_____

_____

_____

_____

_____

_____

_____

_____

_____

_____

_____

_____

_____

Three Moments of Gratitude:

1._____

2._____

3._____

DATE:

THERE'S A POINT WHEN YOU GO WITH WHAT YOU'VE GOT. OR YOU DON'T GO. — JOAN DIDION

Morning:

Three Moments of Gratitude:

1._____

2._____

3._____

Three Worries / Improvements:

1._____

_____

2._____

_____

3._____

_____

Three Things to Accomplish (Mentally or Physically):

1._____

2._____

3._____

Night:

Open Space:

_____

_____

_____

_____

_____

_____

_____

_____

_____

_____

_____

_____

_____

_____

_____

_____

_____

_____

_____

Three Moments of Gratitude:

1._____

2._____

3._____

DATE:

IF YOU ARE NOT WILLING TO RISK THE USUAL, YOU WILL HAVE TO SETTLE FOR THE ORDINARY. — JIM ROHN

Morning:

Three Moments of Gratitude:

1._____

2._____

3._____

Three Worries / Improvements:

1._____

_____

2._____

_____

3._____

_____

Three Things to Accomplish (Mentally or Physically):

1._____

2._____

3._____

Night:

Open Space:

_____

_____

_____

_____

_____

_____

_____

_____

_____

_____

_____

_____

_____

_____

_____

_____

_____

_____

Three Moments of Gratitude:

1._____

2._____

3._____

DATE:

**SOMETIMES IT TAKES A GOOD FALL TO REALLY KNOW WHERE YOU STAND
– HAYLEY WILLIAMS**

Morning:

Three Moments of Gratitude:

1._____

2._____

3._____

Three Worries / Improvements:

1._____

_____

2._____

_____

3._____

_____

Three Things to Accomplish (Mentally or Physically):

1._____

2._____

3._____

Night:

Open Space:

_____

_____

_____

_____

_____

_____

_____

_____

_____

_____

_____

_____

_____

_____

_____

_____

_____

_____

Three Moments of Gratitude:

1._____

2._____

3._____

DATE:

FOCUS ON THE JOURNEY, NOT THE DESTINATION. JOY IS FOUND NOT IN FINISHING AN ACTIVITY BUT IN DOING IT. — GREG ANDERSON

Morning:

Three Moments of Gratitude:

1._____

2._____

3._____

Three Worries / Improvements:

1._____

_____

2._____

_____

3._____

_____

Three Things to Accomplish (Mentally or Physically):

1._____

2._____

3._____

Night:

Open Space:

_____

_____

_____

_____

_____

_____

_____

_____

_____

_____

_____

_____

_____

_____

_____

_____

_____

_____

Three Moments of Gratitude:

1._____

2._____

3._____

DATE:

CHALLENGES ARE WHAT MAKE LIFE INTERESTING AND OVERCOMING THEM IS WHAT MAKES LIFE MEANINGFUL – JOSHUA J. MARINE

Morning:

Three Moments of Gratitude:

1._____

2._____

3._____

Three Worries / Improvements:

1._____

_____

2._____

_____

3._____

_____

Three Things to Accomplish (Mentally or Physically):

1._____

2._____

3._____

Night:

Open Space:

_____

_____

_____

_____

_____

_____

_____

_____

_____

_____

_____

_____

_____

_____

_____

_____

_____

_____

Three Moments of Gratitude:

1._____

2._____

3._____

DATE:

IT AIN'T OVER TILL IT'S OVER — YOGI BERRA

Morning:

Three Moments of Gratitude:

1._____

2._____

3._____

Three Worries / Improvements:

1._____

_____

2._____

_____

3._____

_____

Three Things to Accomplish (Mentally or Physically):

1._____

2._____

3._____

Night:

Open Space:

_____

_____

_____

_____

_____

_____

_____

_____

_____

_____

_____

_____

_____

_____

_____

_____

_____

_____

Three Moments of Gratitude:

1._____

2._____

3._____

DATE:

DO NOT LET WHAT YOU CANNOT DO INTERFERE WITH WHAT YOU CAN DO — JOHN WOODEN

Morning:

Three Moments of Gratitude:

1._____

2._____

3._____

Three Worries / Improvements:

1._____

_____

2._____

_____

3._____

_____

Three Things to Accomplish (Mentally or Physically):

1._____

2._____

3._____

Night:

Open Space:

_____

_____

_____

_____

_____

_____

_____

_____

_____

_____

_____

_____

_____

_____

_____

_____

_____

_____

Three Moments of Gratitude:

1._____

2._____

3._____

DATE:

THE MIND IS EVERYTHING, WHAT YOU THINK YOU BECOME - BUDDA

Morning:

Three Moments of Gratitude:

1._____

2._____

3._____

Three Worries / Improvements:

1._____

_____

2._____

_____

3._____

_____

Three Things to Accomplish (Mentally or Physically):

1._____

2._____

3._____

Night:

Open Space:

_____

_____

_____

_____

_____

_____

_____

_____

_____

_____

_____

_____

_____

_____

_____

_____

_____

_____

Three Moments of Gratitude:

1._____

2._____

3._____

DATE:

THE SECRET OF GETTING AHEAD IS GETTING STARTED — MARK TWAIN

Morning:

Three Moments of Gratitude:

1._____

2._____

3._____

Three Worries / Improvements:

1._____

_____

2._____

_____

3._____

_____

Three Things to Accomplish (Mentally or Physically):

1._____

2._____

3._____

Night:

Open Space:

_____

_____

_____

_____

_____

_____

_____

_____

_____

_____

_____

_____

_____

_____

_____

_____

_____

Three Moments of Gratitude:

1._____

2._____

3._____

DATE:

**FOR SUCCESS, ATTITUDE IS EQUALLY AS IMPORTANT AS ABILITY —
WALTER SCOTT**

Morning:

Three Moments of Gratitude:

1._____

2._____

3._____

Three Worries / Improvements:

1._____

_____

2._____

_____

3._____

_____

Three Things to Accomplish (Mentally or Physically):

1._____

2._____

3._____

Night:

Open Space:

_____

_____

_____

_____

_____

_____

_____

_____

_____

_____

_____

_____

_____

_____

_____

_____

_____

Three Moments of Gratitude:

1._____

2._____

3._____

DATE:

TRUE HAPPINESS IS... TO ENJOY THE PRESENT, WITHOUT ANXIOUS DEPENDENCE UPON THE FUTURE. — LUCIUS ANNAEUS SENECA

Morning:

Three Moments of Gratitude:

1._____

2._____

3._____

Three Worries / Improvements:

1._____

_____

2._____

_____

3._____

_____

Three Things to Accomplish (Mentally or Physically):

1._____

2._____

3._____

Night:

Open Space:

_____

_____

_____

_____

_____

_____

_____

_____

_____

_____

_____

_____

_____

_____

_____

_____

_____

_____

Three Moments of Gratitude:

1._____

2._____

3._____

DATE:

YOU MUST DO THE THING YOU THINK YOU CANNOT DO — ELEANOR ROOSEVELT

Morning:

Three Moments of Gratitude:

1._____

2._____

3._____

Three Worries / Improvements:

1._____

_____

2._____

_____

3._____

_____

Three Things to Accomplish (Mentally or Physically):

1._____

2._____

3._____

Night:

Open Space:

_____

_____

_____

_____

_____

_____

_____

_____

_____

_____

_____

_____

_____

_____

_____

_____

_____

Three Moments of Gratitude:

1._____

2._____

3._____

DATE:

EXPERIENCE IS THE TEACHER OF ALL THINGS — JULIUS CAESAR

Morning:

Three Moments of Gratitude:

1._____

2._____

3._____

Three Worries / Improvements:

1._____

_____

2._____

_____

3._____

_____

Three Things to Accomplish (Mentally or Physically):

1._____

2._____

3._____

Night:

Open Space:

_____

_____

_____

_____

_____

_____

_____

_____

_____

_____

_____

_____

_____

_____

_____

_____

_____

Three Moments of Gratitude:

1._____

2._____

3._____

DATE:

WHEN YOU ARISE IN THE MORNING, THINK OF WHAT A PRECIOUS PRIVILEGE IT IS TO BE ALIVE — TO BREATHE, TO THINK, TO ENJOY, TO LOVE. — MARCUS AURELIUS

Morning:

Three Moments of Gratitude:

1._____

2._____

3._____

Three Worries / Improvements:

1._____

_____

2._____

_____

3._____

_____

Three Things to Accomplish (Mentally or Physically):

1._____

2._____

3._____

Night:

Open Space:

_____

_____

_____

_____

_____

_____

_____

_____

_____

_____

_____

_____

_____

_____

_____

_____

_____

Three Moments of Gratitude:

1._____

2._____

3._____

DATE:

**IF YOU SUFFER, THANK GOD! IT IS A SURE SIGN THAT YOU ARE ALIVE. —
ELBERT HUBBARD**

Morning:

Three Moments of Gratitude:

1._____

2._____

3._____

Three Worries / Improvements:

1._____

_____

2._____

_____

3._____

_____

Three Things to Accomplish (Mentally or Physically):

1._____

2._____

3._____

Night:

Open Space:

_____

_____

_____

_____

_____

_____

_____

_____

_____

_____

_____

_____

_____

_____

_____

_____

_____

_____

Three Moments of Gratitude:

1._____

2._____

3._____

DATE:

SERVICE TO OTHERS IS THE RENT YOU PAY FOR YOUR ROOM HERE ON EARTH — MUHAMMAD ALI

Morning:

Three Moments of Gratitude:

1 _____

2. _____

3. _____

Three Worries / Improvements:

1. _____

_____

2. _____

_____

3. _____

_____

Three Things to Accomplish (Mentally or Physically):

1. _____

2. _____

3. _____

Night:

Open Space:

_____

_____

_____

_____

_____

_____

_____

_____

_____

_____

_____

_____

_____

_____

_____

_____

_____

_____

_____

Three Moments of Gratitude:

1._____

2._____

3._____

DATE:

DON'T JUDGE EACH DAY BY THE HARVEST THAT YOU REAP BUT BY THE SEEDS THAT YOU PLANT. – ROBERT LOUIS STEVENSON

Morning:

Three Moments of Gratitude:

1._____

2._____

3._____

Three Worries / Improvements:

1._____

_____

2._____

_____

3._____

_____

Three Things to Accomplish (Mentally or Physically):

1._____

2._____

3._____

Night:

Open Space:

_____

_____

_____

_____

_____

_____

_____

_____

_____

_____

_____

_____

_____

_____

_____

_____

_____

Three Moments of Gratitude:

1._____

2._____

3._____

DATE:

IF THE WORLD SEEMS COLD TO YOU, KINDLE FIRES TO WARM IT — LUCY LARCOM

Morning:

Three Moments of Gratitude:

1._____

2._____

3._____

Three Worries / Improvements:

1._____

_____

2._____

_____

3._____

_____

Three Things to Accomplish (Mentally or Physically):

1._____

2._____

3._____

Night:

Open Space:

_____

_____

_____

_____

_____

_____

_____

_____

_____

_____

_____

_____

_____

_____

_____

_____

_____

_____

Three Moments of Gratitude:

1._____

2._____

3._____

DATE:

THE SUPERIOR MAN ACTS BEFORE HE SPEAKS, AND AFTERWARDS SPEAKS ACCORDING TO HIS ACTION — CONFUCIUS

Morning:

Three Moments of Gratitude:

1 _____

2. _____

3. _____

Three Worries / Improvements:

1. _____

_____

2. _____

_____

3. _____

_____

Three Things to Accomplish (Mentally or Physically):

1. _____

2. _____

3. _____

Night:

Open Space:

_____

_____

_____

_____

_____

_____

_____

_____

_____

_____

_____

_____

_____

_____

_____

_____

_____

_____

Three Moments of Gratitude:

1._____

2._____

3._____

DATE:

YOU WOULDN'T WORRY SO MUCH ABOUT WHAT OTHERS THINK OF YOU IF YOU REALIZED HOW SELDOM THEY DO — ELEANOR ROOSEVELT

Morning:

Three Moments of Gratitude:

1._____

2._____

3._____

Three Worries / Improvements:

1._____

_____

2._____

_____

3._____

_____

Three Things to Accomplish (Mentally or Physically):

1._____

2._____

3._____

Night:

Open Space:

_____

_____

_____

_____

_____

_____

_____

_____

_____

_____

_____

_____

_____

_____

_____

_____

_____

_____

Three Moments of Gratitude:

1._____

2._____

3._____

DATE:

THERE IS ONLY ONE HAPPINESS IN LIFE, TO LOVE AND BE LOVED — GEORGE SAND

Morning:

Three Moments of Gratitude:

1._____

2._____

3._____

Three Worries / Improvements:

1._____

_____

2._____

_____

3._____

_____

Three Things to Accomplish (Mentally or Physically):

1._____

2._____

3._____

Night:

Open Space:

_____

_____

_____

_____

_____

_____

_____

_____

_____

_____

_____

_____

_____

_____

_____

_____

_____

Three Moments of Gratitude:

1._____

2._____

3._____

DATE:

**OUR DEEDS DETERMINE US, AS MUCH AS WE DETERMINE OUR DEEDS —
GEORGE ELIOT**

Morning:

Three Moments of Gratitude:

1._____

2._____

3._____

Three Worries / Improvements:

1._____

_____

2._____

_____

3._____

_____

Three Things to Accomplish (Mentally or Physically):

1._____

2._____

3._____

Night:

Open Space:

_____

_____

_____

_____

_____

_____

_____

_____

_____

_____

_____

_____

_____

_____

_____

_____

_____

_____

Three Moments of Gratitude:

1._____

2._____

3._____

DATE:

I WANT TO BE ALL I AM CAPABLE OF BECOMING — KATHERINE MANSFIELD

Morning:

Three Moments of Gratitude:

1._____

2._____

3._____

Three Worries / Improvements:

1._____

_____

2._____

_____

3._____

_____

Three Things to Accomplish (Mentally or Physically):

1._____

2._____

3._____

Night:

Open Space:

_____

_____

_____

_____

_____

_____

_____

_____

_____

_____

_____

_____

_____

_____

_____

_____

_____

_____

Three Moments of Gratitude:

1._____

2._____

3._____

DATE:

TRUTH IS SUCH A RARE THING, IT IS DELIGHTFUL TO TELL IT — EMILY DICKINSON

Morning:

Three Moments of Gratitude:

1._____

2._____

3._____

Three Worries / Improvements:

1._____

_____

2._____

_____

3._____

_____

Three Things to Accomplish (Mentally or Physically):

1._____

2._____

3._____

Night:

Open Space:

_____

_____

_____

_____

_____

_____

_____

_____

_____

_____

_____

_____

_____

_____

_____

_____

_____

_____

Three Moments of Gratitude:

1._____

2._____

3._____

DATE:

DARKNESS CAN ONLY BE SCATTERED BY LIGHT, HATRED CAN ONLY BE CONQUERED BY LOVE – ST. JOHN PAUL THE SECOND

Morning:

Three Moments of Gratitude:

1._____

2._____

3._____

Three Worries / Improvements:

1._____

_____

2._____

_____

3._____

_____

Three Things to Accomplish (Mentally or Physically):

1._____

2._____

3._____

Night:

Open Space:

_____

_____

_____

_____

_____

_____

_____

_____

_____

_____

_____

_____

_____

_____

_____

_____

Three Moments of Gratitude:

1._____

2._____

3._____

DATE:

IT'S NOT ABOUT HOW MUCH YOU DO, BUT HOW MUCH LOVE YOU PUT INTO WHAT YOU DO THAT COUNTS – MOTHER TERESA

Morning:

Three Moments of Gratitude:

1._____

2._____

3._____

Three Worries / Improvements:

1._____

_____

2._____

_____

3._____

_____

Three Things to Accomplish (Mentally or Physically):

1._____

2._____

3._____

Night:

Open Space:

_____

_____

_____

_____

_____

_____

_____

_____

_____

_____

_____

_____

_____

_____

_____

_____

Three Moments of Gratitude:

1._____

2._____

3._____

DATE:

I AM THE GREATEST, I SAID THAT EVEN BEFORE I KNEW I WAS — MUHAMMAD ALI

Morning:

Three Moments of Gratitude:

1._____

2._____

3._____

Three Worries / Improvements:

1._____

_____

2._____

_____

3._____

_____

Three Things to Accomplish (Mentally or Physically):

1._____

2._____

3._____

Night:

Open Space:

_____

_____

_____

_____

_____

_____

_____

_____

_____

_____

_____

_____

_____

_____

_____

_____

_____

_____

Three Moments of Gratitude:

1._____

2._____

3._____

DATE:

TO LIVE IS SO STARTLING IT LEAVES LITTLE TIME FOR ANYTHING ELSE – EMILY DICKONSON

Morning:

Three Moments of Gratitude:

1._____

2._____

3._____

Three Worries / Improvements:

1._____

_____

2._____

_____

3._____

_____

Three Things to Accomplish (Mentally or Physically):

1._____

2._____

3._____

Night:

Open Space:

_____

_____

_____

_____

_____

_____

_____

_____

_____

_____

_____

_____

_____

_____

_____

_____

_____

Three Moments of Gratitude:

1._____

2._____

3._____

DATE:

BE FAITHFUL IN SMALL THINGS BECAUSE IT IS IN THEM THAT YOUR STRENGTH LIES – MOTHER THERESA

Morning:

Three Moments of Gratitude:

1._____

2._____

3._____

Three Worries / Improvements:

1._____

_____

2._____

_____

3._____

_____

Three Things to Accomplish (Mentally or Physically):

1._____

2._____

3._____

Night:

Open Space:

_____

_____

_____

_____

_____

_____

_____

_____

_____

_____

_____

_____

_____

_____

_____

_____

_____

Three Moments of Gratitude:

1._____

2._____

3._____

DATE:

WHAT GREAT THING WOULD YOU ATTEMPT IF YOU KNEW YOU COULD NOT FAIL? — ROBERT H. SCHULLER

Morning:

Three Moments of Gratitude:

1._____

2._____

3._____

Three Worries / Improvements:

1._____

_____

2._____

_____

3._____

_____

Three Things to Accomplish (Mentally or Physically):

1._____

2._____

3._____

Night:

Open Space:

_____

_____

_____

_____

_____

_____

_____

_____

_____

_____

_____

_____

_____

_____

_____

_____

_____

Three Moments of Gratitude:

1._____

2._____

3._____

DATE:

USE YOUR HEALTH, EVEN TO THE POINT OF WEARING IT OUT. THAT IS WHAT IT IS FOR. SPEND ALL YOU HAVE BEFORE YOU DIE; DO NOT OUTLIVE YOURSELF — GEORGE DERNARD SHAW

Morning:

Three Moments of Gratitude:

1._____

2._____

3._____

Three Worries / Improvements:

1._____

_____

2._____

_____

3._____

_____

Three Things to Accomplish (Mentally or Physically):

1._____

2._____

3._____

Night:

Open Space:

_____

_____

_____

_____

_____

_____

_____

_____

_____

_____

_____

_____

_____

_____

_____

Three Moments of Gratitude:

1._____

2._____

3._____

DATE:

IF YOU HAVE NO CONFIDENCE IN SELF, YOU ARE TWICE DEFEATED IN THE RACE OF LIFE. WITH CONFIDENCE, YOU HAVE WON EVEN BEFORE YOU HAVE STARTED — CICERO

Morning:

Three Moments of Gratitude:

1._____

2._____

3._____

Three Worries / Improvements:

1._____

_____

2._____

_____

3._____

_____

Three Things to Accomplish (Mentally or Physically):

1._____

2._____

3._____

Night:

Open Space:

_____

_____

_____

_____

_____

_____

_____

_____

_____

_____

_____

_____

_____

_____

_____

_____

Three Moments of Gratitude:

1._____

2._____

3._____

DATE:

A DAY WITHOUT LAUGHTER IS A DAY WASTED — CHARLIE CHAPLIN

Morning:

Three Moments of Gratitude:

1._____

2._____

3._____

Three Worries / Improvements:

1._____

_____

2._____

_____

3._____

_____

Three Things to Accomplish (Mentally or Physically):

1._____

2._____

3._____

Night:

Open Space:

_____

_____

_____

_____

_____

_____

_____

_____

_____

_____

_____

_____

_____

_____

_____

_____

_____

_____

Three Moments of Gratitude:

1._____

2._____

3._____

DATE:

TO MYSELF I AM ONLY A CHILD PLAYING ON THE BEACH, WHILE VAST OCEANS OF TRUTH LIE UNDISCOVERED BEFORE ME – ISSAC NEWTON

Morning:

Three Moments of Gratitude:

1._____

2._____

3._____

Three Worries / Improvements:

1._____

_____

2._____

_____

3._____

_____

Three Things to Accomplish (Mentally or Physically):

1._____

2._____

3._____

Night:

Open Space:

_____

_____

_____

_____

_____

_____

_____

_____

_____

_____

_____

_____

_____

_____

_____

_____

_____

Three Moments of Gratitude:

1._____

2._____

3._____

DATE:

EXPERIENCE IS ONE THING YOU CAN'T GET FOR NOTHING — OSCAR WILDE

Morning:

Three Moments of Gratitude:

1._____

2._____

3._____

Three Worries / Improvements:

1._____

_____

2._____

_____

3._____

_____

Three Things to Accomplish (Mentally or Physically):

1._____

2._____

3._____

Night:

Open Space:

_____

_____

_____

_____

_____

_____

_____

_____

_____

_____

_____

_____

_____

_____

_____

_____

_____

Three Moments of Gratitude:

1._____

2._____

3._____

DATE:

I WANT TO BE ALL USED UP WHEN I DIE — GEORGE BERNARD SHAW

Morning:

Three Moments of Gratitude:

1._____

2._____

3._____

Three Worries / Improvements:

1._____

_____

2._____

_____

3._____

_____

Three Things to Accomplish (Mentally or Physically):

1._____

2._____

3._____

Night:

Open Space:

_____

_____

_____

_____

_____

_____

_____

_____

_____

_____

_____

_____

_____

_____

_____

_____

_____

_____

Three Moments of Gratitude:

1._____

2._____

3._____

DATE:

DO NOT BE SATISFIED WITH MEDIOCRITY. PUT OUT INTO THE DEEP AND LET DOWN YOUR NETS FOR A CATCH. — ST. JOHN PAUL THE SECOND

Morning:

Three Moments of Gratitude:

1._____

2._____

3._____

Three Worries / Improvements:

1._____

_____

2._____

_____

3._____

_____

Three Things to Accomplish (Mentally or Physically):

1._____

2._____

3._____

Night:

Open Space:

_____

_____

_____

_____

_____

_____

_____

_____

_____

_____

_____

_____

_____

_____

_____

_____

_____

Three Moments of Gratitude:

1._____

2._____

3._____

DATE:

IT TAKES COURAGE TO MAKE A FOOL OF YOURSELF — CHARLIE CHAPLIN

Morning:

Three Moments of Gratitude:

1._____

2._____

3._____

Three Worries / Improvements:

1._____

_____

2._____

_____

3._____

_____

Three Things to Accomplish (Mentally or Physically):

1._____

2._____

3._____

Night:

Open Space:

_____

_____

_____

_____

_____

_____

_____

_____

_____

_____

_____

_____

_____

_____

_____

_____

_____

_____

_____

Three Moments of Gratitude:

1._____

2._____

3._____

DATE:

NO MAN IS RICH ENOUGH TO BUY BACK HIS PAST — OSCAR WILDE

Morning:

Three Moments of Gratitude:

1._____

2._____

3._____

Three Worries / Improvements:

1._____

_____

2._____

_____

3._____

_____

Three Things to Accomplish (Mentally or Physically):

1._____

2._____

3._____

Night:

Open Space:

_____

_____

_____

_____

_____

_____

_____

_____

_____

_____

_____

_____

_____

_____

_____

_____

_____

_____

Three Moments of Gratitude:

1._____

2._____

3._____

DATE:

WHAT IS PAST IS PROLOGUE — WILLIAM SHAKESPEARE

Morning:

Three Moments of Gratitude:

1._____

2._____

3._____

Three Worries / Improvements:

1._____

_____

2._____

_____

3._____

_____

Three Things to Accomplish (Mentally or Physically):

1._____

2._____

3._____

Night:

Open Space:

_____

_____

_____

_____

_____

_____

_____

_____

_____

_____

_____

_____

_____

_____

_____

_____

Three Moments of Gratitude:

1._____

2._____

3._____

DATE:

WE FEAR THE FUTURE BECAUSE WE ARE WASTING TODAY — MOTHER
THERESA

Morning:

Three Moments of Gratitude:

1._____

2._____

3._____

Three Worries / Improvements:

1._____

_____

2._____

_____

3._____

_____

Three Things to Accomplish (Mentally or Physically):

1._____

2._____

3._____

Night:

Open Space:

_____

_____

_____

_____

_____

_____

_____

_____

_____

_____

_____

_____

_____

_____

_____

_____

_____

Three Moments of Gratitude:

1._____

2._____

3._____

DATE:

WE THINK TOO MUCH AND FEEL TOO LITTLE – CHARLIE CHAPLIN

Morning:

Three Moments of Gratitude:

1._____

2._____

3._____

Three Worries / Improvements:

1._____

_____

2._____

_____

3._____

_____

Three Things to Accomplish (Mentally or Physically):

1._____

2._____

3._____

Night:

Open Space:

_____

_____

_____

_____

_____

_____

_____

_____

_____

_____

_____

_____

_____

_____

_____

_____

_____

Three Moments of Gratitude:

1._____

2._____

3._____

DATE:

THERE IS NO PLACE FOR SELFISHNESS AND NO PLACE FOR FEAR! DO NOT BE AFRAID, THEN, WHEN LOVE MAKES DEMANDS. DO NOT BE AFRAID WHEN LOVE REQUIRES SACRIFICE — ST. JOHN PAUL THE SECOND

Morning:

Three Moments of Gratitude:

1._____

2._____

3._____

Three Worries / Improvements:

1._____

_____

2._____

_____

3._____

_____

Three Things to Accomplish (Mentally or Physically):

1._____

2._____

3._____

Night:

Open Space:

_____

_____

_____

_____

_____

_____

_____

_____

_____

_____

_____

_____

_____

_____

_____

Three Moments of Gratitude:

1._____

2._____

3._____

DATE:

THE WICKED ENVY AND HATE; IT IS THEIR WAY OF ADMIRING — VICTOR HUGO

Morning:

Three Moments of Gratitude:

1._____

2._____

3._____

Three Worries / Improvements:

1._____

_____

2._____

_____

3._____

_____

Three Things to Accomplish (Mentally or Physically):

1._____

2._____

3._____

Night:

Open Space:

_____

_____

_____

_____

_____

_____

_____

_____

_____

_____

_____

_____

_____

_____

_____

_____

_____

_____

Three Moments of Gratitude:

1._____

2._____

3._____

DATE:

NO ONE CAN MAKE YOU FEEL INFERIOR WITHOUT YOUR CONSENT – ELEANOR ROOSEVELT

Morning:

Three Moments of Gratitude:

1._____

2._____

3._____

Three Worries / Improvements:

1._____

_____

2._____

_____

3._____

_____

Three Things to Accomplish (Mentally or Physically):

1._____

2._____

3._____

Night:

Open Space:

_____
_____
_____
_____
_____
_____
_____
_____
_____
_____
_____
_____
_____
_____
_____
_____
_____
_____

Three Moments of Gratitude:

1._____

2._____

3._____

DATE:

FAILURE IS THE CONDIMENT THAT GIVES SUCCESS ITS FLAVOR – TRUMAN CAPOTE

Morning:

Three Moments of Gratitude:

1._____

2._____

3._____

Three Worries / Improvements:

1._____

_____

2._____

_____

3._____

_____

Three Things to Accomplish (Mentally or Physically):

1._____

2._____

3._____

Night:

Open Space:

_____

_____

_____

_____

_____

_____

_____

_____

_____

_____

_____

_____

_____

_____

_____

_____

_____

Three Moments of Gratitude:

1._____

2._____

3._____

DATE:

DO NOT WAIT TO STRIKE TILL THE IRON IS HOT; BUT MAKE IT HOT BY STRIKING – WILLIAM R. SPRAGUE

Morning:

Three Moments of Gratitude:

1._____

2._____

3._____

Three Worries / Improvements:

1._____

_____

2._____

_____

3._____

_____

Three Things to Accomplish (Mentally or Physically):

1._____

2._____

3._____

Night:

Open Space:

_____

_____

_____

_____

_____

_____

_____

_____

_____

_____

_____

_____

_____

_____

_____

_____

_____

Three Moments of Gratitude:

1._____

2._____

3._____

DATE:

DON'T COUNT THE DAYS; MAKE THE DAYS COUNT. — MUHAMMAD ALI

Morning:

Three Moments of Gratitude:

1._____

2._____

3._____

Three Worries / Improvements:

1._____

_____

2._____

_____

3._____

_____

Three Things to Accomplish (Mentally or Physically):

1._____

2._____

3._____

Night:

Open Space:

_____

_____

_____

_____

_____

_____

_____

_____

_____

_____

_____

_____

_____

_____

_____

_____

_____

_____

Three Moments of Gratitude:

1._____

2._____

3._____

DATE:

SUCCESS IS ACHIEVED BY DEVELOPING OUR STRENGTHS, NOT BY ELIMINATING OUR WEAKNESSES. – MARILYN VOS SAVANT

Morning:

Three Moments of Gratitude:

1._____

2._____

3._____

Three Worries / Improvements:

1._____

_____

2._____

_____

3._____

_____

Three Things to Accomplish (Mentally or Physically):

1._____

2._____

3._____

Night:

Open Space:

_____

_____

_____

_____

_____

_____

_____

_____

_____

_____

_____

_____

_____

_____

_____

_____

Three Moments of Gratitude:

1._____

2._____

3._____

DATE:

NEVER MISTAKE ACTIVITY FOR ACHIEVEMENT — JOHN WOODEN

Morning:

Three Moments of Gratitude:

1._____

2._____

3._____

Three Worries / Improvements:

1._____

_____

2._____

_____

3._____

_____

Three Things to Accomplish (Mentally or Physically):

1._____

2._____

3._____

Night:

Open Space:

_____

_____

_____

_____

_____

_____

_____

_____

_____

_____

_____

_____

_____

_____

_____

_____

_____

Three Moments of Gratitude:

1._____

2._____

3._____

DATE:

YOUR TRUE CHARACTER IS MOST ACCURATELY MEASURED BY HOW YOU TREAT THOSE WHO CAN DO 'NOTHING' FOR YOU – MOTHER THERESA

Morning:

Three Moments of Gratitude:

1._____

2._____

3._____

Three Worries / Improvements:

1._____

_____

2._____

_____

3._____

_____

Three Things to Accomplish (Mentally or Physically):

1._____

2._____

3._____

Night:

Open Space:

_____
_____
_____
_____
_____
_____
_____
_____
_____
_____
_____
_____
_____
_____
_____
_____
_____

Three Moments of Gratitude:

1._____

2._____

3._____

DATE:

YOU CAN'T BUILD A REPUTATION ON WHAT YOU'RE GOING TO DO — HENRY FORD

Morning:

Three Moments of Gratitude:

1._____

2._____

3._____

Three Worries / Improvements:

1._____

_____

2._____

_____

3._____

_____

Three Things to Accomplish (Mentally or Physically):

1._____

2._____

3._____

Night:

Open Space:

_____

_____

_____

_____

_____

_____

_____

_____

_____

_____

_____

_____

_____

_____

_____

_____

_____

Three Moments of Gratitude:

1._____

2._____

3._____

DATE:

DO ONE THING EVERY DAY THAT SCARES YOU — ELEANOR ROOSEVELT

Morning:

Three Moments of Gratitude:

1._____

2._____

3._____

Three Worries / Improvements:

1._____

_____

2._____

_____

3._____

_____

Three Things to Accomplish (Mentally or Physically):

1._____

2._____

3._____

Night:

Open Space:

_____

_____

_____

_____

_____

_____

_____

_____

_____

_____

_____

_____

_____

_____

_____

_____

Three Moments of Gratitude:

1._____

2._____

3._____

DATE:

**LIFE ISN'T ABOUT FINDING YOURSELF. LIFE IS ABOUT CREATING YOURSELF.
— GEORGE BERNARD SHAW**

Morning:

Three Moments of Gratitude:

1._____

2._____

3._____

Three Worries / Improvements:

1._____

_____

2._____

_____

3._____

_____

Three Things to Accomplish (Mentally or Physically):

1._____

2._____

3._____

Night:

Open Space:

_____

_____

_____

_____

_____

_____

_____

_____

_____

_____

_____

_____

_____

_____

_____

Three Moments of Gratitude:

1._____

2._____

3._____

DATE:

LIFE IS NEVER FAIR, AND PERHAPS IT IS A GOOD THING FOR MOST OF US THAT IT IS NOT. — OSCAR WILDE

Morning:

Three Moments of Gratitude:

1._____

2._____

3._____

Three Worries / Improvements:

1._____

_____

2._____

_____

3._____

_____

Three Things to Accomplish (Mentally or Physically):

1._____

2._____

3._____

Night:

Open Space:

_____

_____

_____

_____

_____

_____

_____

_____

_____

_____

_____

_____

_____

_____

_____

_____

Three Moments of Gratitude:

1._____

2._____

3._____

DATE:

THOU WILT FINDREST FROM VAIN FANCIES IF THOU DOEST EVERY ACT IN LIFE AS THOUGH IT WERE THY LAST – ARISTOTLE

Morning:

Three Moments of Gratitude:

1._____

2._____

3._____

Three Worries / Improvements:

1._____

_____

2._____

_____

3._____

_____

Three Things to Accomplish (Mentally or Physically):

1._____

2._____

3._____

Night:

Open Space:

_____

_____

_____

_____

_____

_____

_____

_____

_____

_____

_____

_____

_____

_____

_____

_____

_____

_____

_____

Three Moments of Gratitude:

1._____

2._____

3._____

DATE:

A LIFE SPENT MAKING MISTAKES IS NOT ONLY MORE HONORABLE, BUT MORE USEFUL THAN A LIFE SPENT DOING NOTHING — GEORGE BERNARD SHAW

Morning:

Three Moments of Gratitude:

1._____

2._____

3._____

Three Worries / Improvements:

1._____

_____

2._____

_____

3._____

_____

Three Things to Accomplish (Mentally or Physically):

1._____

2._____

3._____

Night:

Open Space:

_____

_____

_____

_____

_____

_____

_____

_____

_____

_____

_____

_____

_____

_____

_____

_____

_____

_____

Three Moments of Gratitude:

1._____

2._____

3._____

DATE:

ONLY A LIFE LIVED FOR OTHERS IS A LIFE WORTHWHILE — ALBERT EINSTEIN

Morning:

Three Moments of Gratitude:

1._____

2._____

3._____

Three Worries / Improvements:

1._____

_____

2._____

_____

3._____

_____

Three Things to Accomplish (Mentally or Physically):

1._____

2._____

3._____

Night:

Open Space:

_____

_____

_____

_____

_____

_____

_____

_____

_____

_____

_____

_____

_____

_____

_____

Three Moments of Gratitude:

1._____

2._____

3._____

DATE:

ONE SHOULD SYMPATHISE WITH THE COLOUR, THE BEAUTY, THE JOY OF LIFE. THE LESS SAID ABOUT LIFE'S SORES THE BETTER — OSCAR WILDE

Morning:

Three Moments of Gratitude:

1._____

2._____

3._____

Three Worries / Improvements:

1._____

_____

2._____

_____

3._____

_____

Three Things to Accomplish (Mentally or Physically):

1._____

2._____

3._____

Night:

Open Space:

_____

_____

_____

_____

_____

_____

_____

_____

_____

_____

_____

_____

_____

_____

_____

_____

_____

_____

Three Moments of Gratitude:

1._____

2._____

3._____

DATE:

**LIFE IS REALLY SIMPLE, BUT WE INSIST ON MAKING IT COMPLICATED —
CONFUCIUS**

Morning:

Three Moments of Gratitude:

1._____

2._____

3._____

Three Worries / Improvements:

1._____

_____

2._____

_____

3._____

_____

Three Things to Accomplish (Mentally or Physically):

1._____

2._____

3._____

Night:

Open Space:

_____

_____

_____

_____

_____

_____

_____

_____

_____

_____

_____

_____

_____

_____

_____

_____

_____

Three Moments of Gratitude:

1._____

2._____

3._____

DATE:

STRIVE NOT TO BE A SUCCESS, BUT RATHER TO BE OF VALUE. — ALBERT EINSTEIN

Morning:

Three Moments of Gratitude:

1._____

2._____

3._____

Three Worries / Improvements:

1._____

_____

2._____

_____

3._____

_____

Three Things to Accomplish (Mentally or Physically):

1._____

2._____

3._____

Night:

Open Space:

_____

_____

_____

_____

_____

_____

_____

_____

_____

_____

_____

_____

_____

_____

_____

_____

Three Moments of Gratitude:

1._____

2._____

3._____

DATE:

SUCCESS IS OFTEN ACHIEVED BY THOSE WHO DON'T KNOW THAT FAILURE IS INEVITABLE – COCO CHANEL

Morning:

Three Moments of Gratitude:

1._____

2._____

3._____

Three Worries / Improvements:

1._____

_____

2._____

_____

3._____

_____

Three Things to Accomplish (Mentally or Physically):

1._____

2._____

3._____

Night:

Open Space:

_____

_____

_____

_____

_____

_____

_____

_____

_____

_____

_____

_____

_____

_____

_____

_____

_____

_____

Three Moments of Gratitude:

1._____

2._____

3._____

DATE:

BEFORE EVERYTHING ELSE, GETTING READY IS THE SECRET OF SUCCESS – HENRY FORD

Morning:

Three Moments of Gratitude:

1._____

2._____

3._____

Three Worries / Improvements:

1._____

_____

2._____

_____

3._____

_____

Three Things to Accomplish (Mentally or Physically):

1._____

2._____

3._____

Night:

Open Space:

_____

_____

_____

_____

_____

_____

_____

_____

_____

_____

_____

_____

_____

_____

_____

_____

_____

_____

Three Moments of Gratitude:

1._____

2._____

3._____

DATE:

I MAY BE NO BETTER, BUT AT LEAST I AM DIFFERENT — JEAN JACQUES ROUSSEAU

Morning:

Three Moments of Gratitude:

1._____

2._____

3._____

Three Worries / Improvements:

1._____

_____

2._____

_____

3._____

_____

Three Things to Accomplish (Mentally or Physically):

1._____

2._____

3._____

Night:

Open Space:

_____

_____

_____

_____

_____

_____

_____

_____

_____

_____

_____

_____

_____

_____

_____

_____

_____

Three Moments of Gratitude:

1._____

2._____

3._____

DATE:

DON'T FIND FAULT, FIND A REMEDY. — HENRY FORD

Morning:

Three Moments of Gratitude:

1._____

2._____

3._____

Three Worries / Improvements:

1._____

_____

2._____

_____

3._____

_____

Three Things to Accomplish (Mentally or Physically):

1._____

2._____

3._____

Night:

Open Space:

_____

_____

_____

_____

_____

_____

_____

_____

_____

_____

_____

_____

_____

_____

_____

_____

_____

Three Moments of Gratitude:

1._____

2._____

3._____

DATE:

LEARN FROM YESTERDAY, LIVE FOR TODAY, HOPE FOR TOMORROW. THE IMPORTANT THING IS NOT TO STOP QUESTIONING. — ALBERT EINSTEIN

Morning:

Three Moments of Gratitude:

1._____

2._____

3._____

Three Worries / Improvements:

1._____

_____

2._____

_____

3._____

_____

Three Things to Accomplish (Mentally or Physically):

1._____

2._____

3._____

Night:

Open Space:

_____

_____

_____

_____

_____

_____

_____

_____

_____

_____

_____

_____

_____

_____

_____

_____

_____

Three Moments of Gratitude:

1._____

2._____

3._____

DATE:

TO LIVE WITHOUT HOPE IS TO CEASE TO LIVE — FIODOR MIHAILOVICI DOSTOEVSKI

Morning:

Three Moments of Gratitude:

1._____

2._____

3._____

Three Worries / Improvements:

1._____

_____

2._____

_____

3._____

_____

Three Things to Accomplish (Mentally or Physically):

1._____

2._____

3._____

Night:

Open Space:

_____

_____

_____

_____

_____

_____

_____

_____

_____

_____

_____

_____

_____

_____

_____

_____

_____

_____

Three Moments of Gratitude:

1._____

2._____

3._____

DATE:

WE ARE AFRAID OF THE ENORMITY OF THE POSSIBLE — EMIL CIORAN

Morning:

Three Moments of Gratitude:

1._____

2._____

3._____

Three Worries / Improvements:

1._____

_____

2._____

_____

3._____

_____

Three Things to Accomplish (Mentally or Physically):

1._____

2._____

3._____

Night:

Open Space:

_____

_____

_____

_____

_____

_____

_____

_____

_____

_____

_____

_____

_____

_____

_____

_____

_____

Three Moments of Gratitude:

1._____

2._____

3._____

DATE:

WE MUST ACCEPT FINITE DISAPPOINTMENT, BUT NEVER LOSE INFINITE HOPE – MARTIN LUTHER KING JR.

Morning:

Three Moments of Gratitude:

1._____

2._____

3._____

Three Worries / Improvements:

1._____

_____

2._____

_____

3._____

_____

Three Things to Accomplish (Mentally or Physically):

1._____

2._____

3._____

Night:

Open Space:

_____

_____

_____

_____

_____

_____

_____

_____

_____

_____

_____

_____

_____

_____

_____

_____

_____

_____

Three Moments of Gratitude:

1._____

2._____

3._____

DATE:

NECESSITY IS THE MOTHER OF TAKING CHANCES — MARK TWAIN

Morning:

Three Moments of Gratitude:

1._____

2._____

3._____

Three Worries / Improvements:

1._____

_____

2._____

_____

3._____

_____

Three Things to Accomplish (Mentally or Physically):

1._____

2._____

3._____

Night:

Open Space:

_____

_____

_____

_____

_____

_____

_____

_____

_____

_____

_____

_____

_____

_____

_____

_____

_____

_____

Three Moments of Gratitude:

1._____

2._____

3._____

DATE:

HONESTY IS THE FIRST CHAPTER IN THE BOOK OF WISDOM — THOMAS JEFFERSON

Morning:

Three Moments of Gratitude:

1._____

2._____

3._____

Three Worries / Improvements:

1._____

_____

2._____

_____

3._____

_____

Three Things to Accomplish (Mentally or Physically):

1._____

2._____

3._____

Night:

Open Space:

_____

_____

_____

_____

_____

_____

_____

_____

_____

_____

_____

_____

_____

_____

_____

_____

_____

_____

Three Moments of Gratitude:

1._____

2._____

3._____

DATE:

OBSTACLES ARE THOSE FRIGHTFUL THINGS YOU SEE WHEN YOU TAKE YOUR EYES OFF YOUR GOAL – HENRY FORD

Morning:

Three Moments of Gratitude:

1._____

2._____

3._____

Three Worries / Improvements:

1._____

_____

2._____

_____

3._____

_____

Three Things to Accomplish (Mentally or Physically):

1._____

2._____

3._____

Night:

Open Space:

_____

_____

_____

_____

_____

_____

_____

_____

_____

_____

_____

_____

_____

_____

_____

_____

_____

_____

Three Moments of Gratitude:

1._____

2._____

3._____

DATE:

LISTEN TO MANY, SPEAK TO A FEW. — WILLIAM SHAKESPEARE

Morning:

Three Moments of Gratitude:

1._____

2._____

3._____

Three Worries / Improvements:

1._____

_____

2._____

_____

3._____

_____

Three Things to Accomplish (Mentally or Physically):

1._____

2._____

3._____

Night:

Open Space:

_____

_____

_____

_____

_____

_____

_____

_____

_____

_____

_____

_____

_____

_____

_____

_____

_____

Three Moments of Gratitude:

1._____

2._____

3._____

DATE:

BE KIND WHENEVER POSSIBLE. IT IS ALWAYS POSSIBLE. — DALAI LAMA

Morning:

Three Moments of Gratitude:

1._____

2._____

3._____

Three Worries / Improvements:

1._____

_____

2._____

_____

3._____

_____

Three Things to Accomplish (Mentally or Physically):

1._____

2._____

3._____

Night:

Open Space:

_____

_____

_____

_____

_____

_____

_____

_____

_____

_____

_____

_____

_____

_____

_____

_____

_____

Three Moments of Gratitude:

1._____

2._____

3._____

DATE:

A DAY WASTED ON OTHERS IS NOT WASTED ON ONE'S SELF. — CHARLES DICKENS

Morning:

Three Moments of Gratitude:

1._____

2._____

3._____

Three Worries / Improvements:

1._____

_____

2._____

_____

3._____

_____

Three Things to Accomplish (Mentally or Physically):

1._____

2._____

3._____

Night:

Open Space:

_____

_____

_____

_____

_____

_____

_____

_____

_____

_____

_____

_____

_____

_____

_____

_____

_____

Three Moments of Gratitude:

1._____

2._____

3._____

DATE:

THE ONLY THING THAT SHOULD SURPRISE US IS THAT THERE ARE STILL SOME THINGS THAT CAN SURPRISE US. – FRANCOIS DE LA ROCHEFOUCAULD

Morning:

Three Moments of Gratitude:

1._____

2._____

3._____

Three Worries / Improvements:

1._____

_____

2._____

_____

3._____

_____

Three Things to Accomplish (Mentally or Physically):

1._____

2._____

3._____

Night:

Open Space:

_____

_____

_____

_____

_____

_____

_____

_____

_____

_____

_____

_____

_____

_____

_____

_____

_____

_____

Three Moments of Gratitude:

1._____

2._____

3._____

DATE:

IF A MAN HAS ANY GREATNESS IN HIM, IT COMES TO LIGHT, NOT IN ONE FLAMBOYANT HOUR, BUT IN THE LEDGER OF HIS DAILY WORK. — BERYL MARKHAM

Morning:

Three Moments of Gratitude:

1._____

2._____

3._____

Three Worries / Improvements:

1._____

_____

2._____

_____

3._____

_____

Three Things to Accomplish (Mentally or Physically):

1._____

2._____

3._____

Night:

Open Space:

_____

_____

_____

_____

_____

_____

_____

_____

_____

_____

_____

_____

_____

_____

_____

_____

_____

_____

Three Moments of Gratitude:

1._____

2._____

3._____

DATE:

THE GRASS MAY SEEM GREENER ON THE OTHER SIDE, BUT YOUR GRASS IS PRETTY DANG GREEN — SEAN DUFFY

Morning:

Three Moments of Gratitude:

1._____

2._____

3._____

Three Worries / Improvements:

1._____

_____

2._____

_____

3._____

_____

Three Things to Accomplish (Mentally or Physically):

1._____

2._____

3._____

Night:

Open Space:

_____

_____

_____

_____

_____

_____

_____

_____

_____

_____

_____

_____

_____

_____

_____

_____

_____

Three Moments of Gratitude:

1._____

2._____

3._____

DATE:

YESTERDAY IS GONE. TOMORROW HAS NOT YET COME. WE HAVE ONLY TODAY. — MOTHER TERESA

Morning:

Three Moments of Gratitude:

1._____

2._____

3._____

Three Worries / Improvements:

1._____

_____

2._____

_____

3._____

_____

Three Things to Accomplish (Mentally or Physically):

1._____

2._____

3._____

Night:

Open Space:

_____

_____

_____

_____

_____

_____

_____

_____

_____

_____

_____

_____

_____

_____

_____

_____

_____

Three Moments of Gratitude:

1._____

2._____

3._____

About the Author

My name is Karina Duffy, and I am an 18-year-old daughter of Christ. I am in love with Catholicism, my family and friends, the city of Chicago, and reading books about neuroscience. You can catch me working out with other empowering women/men at the YMCA, browsing through thrift stores, scouting new places to eat on Yelp, laughing with friends, and spending time at Padre Serra Parish praying the rosary & sharing my faith with others. I live in Camarillo, CA with my two parents and brother. I will be attending the University of Notre Dame. I plan on double majoring in Neuroscience & Behavior and Theology. I try my best to savor the simple moments and approach everything with love & humility.

If you would like a prayer request or to contact me for any reason, my email is karinaduffy3@gmail.com

If you want to see a peek of my crazy, blessed life or updates for where this journal goes, follow me on Instagram @karinaduffyy

Made in the USA
Coppell, TX
15 September 2020